Letters out of Africa

A story of ordinary people called
to do the extraordinary for God

Suzanne Montgomery M.D.

Table of Contents

Preface
Chapter 1
Chapter 2
Chapter 3
Chapter 4
Chapter 5
Chapter 6
Chapter 7
Chapter 8
Chapter 9
Chapter 10
Chapter 11
Chapter 12
Chapter 13
Chapter 14
Chapter 15
Chapter 16
Epilogue
Acknowledgement
Study Questions
Resources
About the Author

Preface

"Letters Out of Africa" is a work orchestrated by the hand of God. If not for God's direct intervention, none of what I am relaying in this book would have been possible. Sometimes God does the impossible to get our attention. The Lord knows that He often needs a sledgehammer to get mine. My hope is that those that take the time to read these pages will grasp the magnitude of what God can and does do through each and every one of us if we are willing. The willingness on our part is the hard part, but oh what an exciting journey is ahead if we say yes to God.

Chapter 1

I had been feeling a sense of restlessness for some time now. I couldn't quite put my finger on why or what it meant. I certainly have had a full life with a husband, three children, two dogs and a cat plus a full time medical practice. Makes you tired just to think about it. I was busy but I had this sense that I needed to be doing more. Not really that I needed to be doing more but that God wanted me to do more. But what? This was the part I didn't know and it bothered me. I was active at church serving on various committees and even doing some mission work locally. All this though didn't seem to be what He wanted. I prayed, "What is it you want me to do, Lord?" He didn't answer. I waited. "Show me what you want me to do, Lord. I'm open and willing to do what you want." Now this is a very dangerous prayer but I didn't realize it at the time. I know now that when a person truly opens their heart to God's will, He will ask you to do things that very likely will be out of your comfort zone. I didn't know it yet but that's exactly what He had in mind for me. He was already setting things up across an ocean in the small country of Liberia to accomplish what He wanted me to do. Now I just had to wait until His timing was right.

Chapter 2

The adventure God had planned for me started on what seemed to be an ordinary Sunday morning. We had rushed around trying to get three children ready for church and as usual we were late. I didn't know ahead of time that we were going to have a guest speaker in the pulpit that morning. Her name was Caroline Wagner and she was speaking about Operation Classroom, a mission of the Methodist Church that runs schools in West Africa. She and her husband, Joe were the Indiana directors of Operation Classroom. They had just returned from a trip to Africa to inspect one of the schools in the Ivory Coast that was educating young people who were refugees from war torn Liberia that neighbors the Ivory Coast. I'd heard of Operation Classroom before and I already knew much of what they did but even so I had a nudging from God. "Listen to what she is saying." As she was telling about their trip, she began to tell of a young man who had great promise. She was sad that it appeared he would have no chance to get higher education after he graduated high school there in the Ivory Coast.
She didn't mention the young man's name or even what he wanted to do with his life but at that moment I felt a sensation I'd never felt before. I knew distinctly that God's Spirit was present there in the church with me. Yes, I know that God is present with us always but this was different. I could feel the weight of unseen hands on my shoulders and a voice spoke to my heart. "This is what I want you to do. You can help this young man." At that moment I knew with certainty this was not coming from me. This was undeniably God. He was answering my prayer in a powerful and a bit scary way. I was awestruck. Was anyone else feeling the way I was? I looked around me. Nothing was different from the usual Sunday morning service. God had just decided to visit me in the middle of my ordinary day.
The question now was what to do about this extra ordinary experience. After the service ended, I was hurriedly trying to round up my three little ones. Carolyn was leaving the church! I had to speak with her. I caught up with her in the parking lot. I heard myself saying, "Can you tell me more about this promising young man? I think I might be able to help." I gave her my name and contact information and she said she would get back with me. I couldn't help but feeling, "Are you crazy or what?"
Months went by and I heard nothing. "God, are you sure this is what

you want me to do? I did my part but I'm not getting any response." No direct answer this time so I waited. I didn't realize then how long it takes for communication back and forth from Africa. This was the early '90's. There were very few phones to this area in the Ivory Coast and email was virtually nonexistent. It took months but I finally received a letter, not just from Carolyn but it included a letter from him.

His name was Shadrach. I'd never known anyone by the name of Shadrach except in the Book of Daniel. He was one of Daniel's three friends, Shadrach, Meshach and Abednego. They had all been thrown in the fiery furnace because they wouldn't worship the golden statue that King Nebuchadnezzar set up. With great courage they said to the king, "If our God whom we serve is able to deliver us from the furnace of blazing fire and out of your hand, O king, let him deliver us. But if not, be it known to you, O king, that we will not serve your gods and we will not worship the golden statue you have set up." 1 They were saved from the king, walked through the fiery furnace, and lived. I imagined that this modern day Shadrach had already walked through more than his fair share of fire at a young age and was a survivor. His letter began a story of survival that I would come to know in the months ahead.

Protestant Methodist Resource Center
Danane', Cote D'ivoire (Ivory Coast)

November 5, 1993

A PERSONAL STATEMENT

I am Shadrach G.N. Gonqueh, a Liberian by nationality. I am the 3rd child in a family of 9 children (four boys, five girls). I was raised in a loving Christian household. My father has served as a laborer of the Firestone Plantation Company- a job that barely gave us enough to eat with no savings for our future educational pursuits. He served this post for 20 years until the outbreak of the civil war on December 24, 1989.

My mother is a devoted and loving housewife and mother. Because of her limited educational achievements, she has been unable to engage in gainful employment.

The bulk of my early years were spent on the Firestone Plantation Company. I attended the Firestone Plantation Public School System until the completion of the 9th grade. Throughout my school years, I've always been a high achiever (an A student). I was greatly encouraged by my parents to be the best that I could be (spiritually, morally and academically) and I've still been driven by that encouragement today.

Because of my good performance in school, I was offered a senior high school scholarship by the Firestone Plantation. With this scholarship I enrolled in the BWJ vocational training institution in Liberia. I chose this institution because I perceived my parent's inability to finance my college education. I felt that if I was equipped with some vocational training I would have a better chance of finding a job and thereby save money to sponsor myself through college. Unfortunately, my educational career at the vocational training school was interrupted by the present civil war in our country. During the war, my family sought refuge in my father's home, a small village called Saclepea located in northeastern Liberia. During the ceasefire I enrolled in a Methodist Mission School in Ganta, Liberia and completed part of my senior high school requirements. In October 1992, there was a resurgence of fighting in Liberia. All schools were again closed. In an effort to complete my senior high level education, I traveled to Danane', Cote D'Ivoire as I'd heard that a senior high level refugee school was opened for Liberian refugees residing in Danane'.

I am interested both in theological and medical studies. My interest in theology has been (and continues to be) influenced by the still soft voice(s) I repeatedly hear from the following scriptures: Mt. 28:18-19, Mk. 8:36, Mk. 16:15-16, etc. God has made it clear to me since my rebirth in April 1980 that he has called me to preach his word to the many dying souls in the world. To make this clear, he has given me the talents I need to do what He wants me do- "Thanks Be to God." My desire to study medicine upon graduation has also been influenced by the growing demands for hospitals and trained medical personnel who would be willing to go out to the rural areas of our country where these medical facilities are poorly staffed and almost nonexistent. It is my sincere and prayerful desire to serve my people...especially those in the rural areas, for they suffer greatly. As a victim of poverty, I fully understand the need for qualified and dedicated role models to serve Liberia's rural citizenry.

With high hopes in God and his word, believing that the world and all its fullness belong to Him and His children of whom I'm part, I trust that these dreams will be realized to His own glory.

Shadrach

I was awestruck by his letter. A doctor! He wants to be a doctor! Carolyn hadn't even mentioned this in her talk at church that day months ago. God knew. He was matching two people on different continents from different cultures who had like goals to serve His purposes. I was willing but a little scared. My next step-to get to know this young man named Shadrach.

1Daniel 3:17-18 from The New Oxford Annotated Bible, 1994

Chapter 3

Shadrach's first letter introducing himself barely touched on the horror he and his family had endured. Life as he knew it had been totally shattered by the civil war that started in 1989 and would extend to 1996. Though poor by the world's standards, life before the war was at least stable. His family lived on the Firestone Plantation where rubber was harvested to be used in the making of tires and other rubber products. This was home for Shadrach and his 8 siblings. He was a gifted student and had hopes for a higher education through a scholarship by Firestone. When the war broke out that education ceased. In fact it was dangerous to be educated. The soldiers would target the educated because they were a threat. The rebels would capture children and make them into soldiers. During the war, it was estimated that there were 60,000 rebel fighters, 60% of these were child soldiers. Ten percent of the population of Liberia were murdered, most of them civilians. Of the rest, ¾ of the population were displaced people or refugees. Women and girls fared the worst. They were raped and murdered with impunity by all of the warring factions.[2]
Shadrach would later tell stories of this time in his life. Many of them told of how God intervened to save he and his family. On one such occasion he and his mother, Ruth were walking back home from another village in the evening. As was often their way, they were singing with each other. They safely reached their destination, not knowing the danger they had been in. Shadrach would be told later by an ex-soldier that he and others lay in wait for him that night. They did not attack because they heard so many voices singing that they thought he was with a crowd of people, not just his mother. When Shadrach told this man that he and his mother were alone, he was incredulous. He thought an army was with them. Shadrach could only give credit to God at that moment for he knew that it must have been an army of angels singing with he and his mother that night that saved them. Another time when he was traveling with some other students, they were stopped at a rebel checkpoint. There was a long line to get through the checkpoint so he and his friends were able to observe what was happening. The soldiers were detaining the people from Nimba county where Shadrach lived. It was obvious that they intended to harm them. His friends knew that Shadrach very likely was going to be killed if he stayed in the line for the checkpoint. They were not from Nimba county but were willing to

help him escape. They devised a plan to divert the attention of the soldiers so that Shadrach could get away by running into the jungle. They started their diversion and Shadrach began to run. It wasn't long until the soldiers saw what was happening and they began to shoot at him. He could feel the bullets going by but was able to reach the jungle unharmed. He walked in the jungle several days before he was able to make his way home. God had saved him again.

During this time, it became so dangerous that his family fled into the jungle and lived on what they could find to eat. His mother was often the last person to eat anything so the children would have enough. They vowed then to all survive or die together. By the end of the civil war, Shadrach's whole family had made it through and none of the children were conscripted to be child soldiers. This was a miracle itself.

It was when Shadrach and his sister, Mary traveled to the Ivory Coast to attend the refugee school there, that he was to meet more angels of God that would help him along the path God was leading him. Two of those people were Reverend Zigbou and his wife Mary. He was a native born Liberian and she an American. Together they ran the refugee school in Danane', Ivory Coast. Shadrach has great respect and fondness for both of these mentors. Rev. Zigbou was the one to hold up a high standard for Shadrach and move him to better himself. Mary was more of a surrogate mother to him, protecting him as she would her own children They were both instrumental in Shadrach meeting Carolyn and Joe Wagner of Operation Classroom setting into motion the events that would bring Shadrach and I together in a special friendship ordained and orchestrated by God himself.

2"The Year the Locust Have Eaten: Liberia 1816-2004" by Joseph Tellewoyan

Chapter 4

Having the desire and the means to help Shadrach further his education and actually accomplishing this were two vastly different things. I was about to go through a difficult journey with Shadrach, trying to achieve this goal. Some days it seemed impossible. To keep going forward we had to continue reminding ourselves that with God all things are possible. The first hurdle was the choice of school. In an initial letter from Carolyn Wagner, she warned against Shadrach coming to the United States for his college education.

November 22, 1993

> *...Although Shadrach doesn't mention just what specific college or university he hopes to attend, I would hope that it would be in West Africa and not in the United States. We strongly advise against bringing undergraduates to the US for several reasons; one a very practical one: a student can receive a reasonably good college education in West Africa at a tiny fraction of the cost of college in the States (4 years in W.A. would be cheaper than 1 in the US!). Also, visas to come from West Africa to the States to study are difficult to come by these days; a large percentage never return home, which contributes to the "brain drain" of these countries who need their talented young people if they're going to have any kind of national future. Postgraduate study is another matter, but a discussion of that is not relevant at this stage of Shadrach's educational career...*

Carolyn Wagner

Given this information from Carolyn, I felt that I needed to be careful what I promised to Shadrach. I determined that my letter back to him would need to strongly encourage him to apply to West African universities. In this way, I could help him with his education but also ensure that he would stay in Liberia. There was no way for me to know how dedicated he was to return to help his own people once he experienced American life.

January 23, 1994

Dear Shadrach,

Carolyn Wagner has so kindly forwarded your autobiography to me. She has spoken highly of your talent and your desire for higher education. I noted your interest in medicine and the ministry, two fields both challenging and greatly needed in your country. I'm sure your family and the people of your community would be both proud and thankful for one of their own to help them by becoming a healer of their bodies as well as their souls.
I myself am a Family Physician in Indianapolis. We are a city with just under one million people. My practice consists of a variety of socioeconomic classes and races. I also volunteer my time giving free medical care to the homeless of our community. I am married and have three children ages 10, 7, and 5. I have been a member of Christ United Methodist of Westfield, Indiana since I was a child. This is where I heard Carolyn Wagner speak of Operation Classroom. My minister, David Owen and his wife June, have also been involved in this program. They will be returning to Liberia in February to train counselors to deal with the psychological trauma of the recent war. I have often thought of entering the mission field through work like this. However, God has shown me through his quiet persuasion that my ministry for now is here. He does continue to open up doors that enable me to help others.
This is the reason for my letter to you. I feel that God has blessed me with the means to help further your education. I understand that there are excellent opportunities for undergraduate education there in West Africa. Have you applied to any schools yet? I would be willing to help sponsor you there on a yearly basis. If your grades proved your commitment, I would continue the sponsorship.
Please let me know what your specific plans are for the future. Carolyn Wagner has indicated that she can direct me as to the logistics of how to help you accomplish them.

Sincerely,
Suzanne Montgomery

My minister, David Owen hand carried my letter to Monrovia, Liberia and gave it to Mary and Herbert Zigbou to take to Shadrach who remained in Danane', Ivory Coast. Mary sent her greetings from Liberia and gave me encouragement that Shadrach might be able to attend university in Monrovia.

Monrovia, Liberia

March 8, 1994

> *...I am going to encourage Shadrach to come to Monrovia, Liberia and attend the University of Liberia's Medical School. The university has been rocky since the war. There was much damage, and its academic program has been off and on due to lack of funding. However, with the seating (March 7) of the new caretaker government in Liberia, there are sure signs of financial reconstruction assistance to Liberia. This has been stalled because of the dubious political stability during the past 4 years...*

Mary Zigbou

My hopes and prayers were for Shadrach's safe arrival in Monrovia and that he would be able with the help of the Zigbou's to enroll in the university there to pursue his studies. I sent money through the Zigbou's to help Shadrach with expenses for travel, tuition and room and board at the school. Unfortunately, the civil war again prevented this.

Monrovia, Liberia

July 9, 1994

> *...Since my arrival, I've tried auditing some courses at the Liberian University including English 101, Chemisty 102, Biology 102, Physics 105 and Pre-Calculus 107. It is however, important to note that everything at the university (as well as in the entire country) is out of order. There are at least a hundred students in each of the small classes and one must rush for a seat or stand during class time. Teachers are always on and off because they aren't being paid and many have left their jobs thereby leaving their classes without a professor. Moreover, for a science (biology and chemistry) major like me, there isn't any laboratory equip-*

ment to be found. Everything was looted during the war which still has a great psychological effect on all the students. Classes are therefore taught on a mere theoretical basis. Because of all the unpreparedness for operation, the university has ruled out graduating anyone until the country is settled...

Shadrach

With this information, it became apparent that pursuring an education in Monrovia would be impossible at this time. Thus began our search for a university in the United States for Shadrach and the ordeal it would be to get a visa from the US Embassy in Monrovia.

Chapter 5

The level of frustration and anxiety that Shadrach was feeling during this time of trying to get him into an American university was very evident in his letters. It was difficult to comfort or console him with one obstacle after another blocking his way. First he had to sit for the TOFLE, a test of English as a foreign language. He did exceptionally well on this since the primary language spoken in Liberia is English. He sent applications to several US schools and was awaiting response when fighting broke out again in Liberia.

Monrovia, Liberia

September 15, 1994

...I woke up early this morning and after my morning devotion decided to turn on our national radio station and monitor the happenings around. To my amazement, the radio station was down. Confused, I got ready and decided to travel to the school where I had been auditing upon my arrival in Monrovia. I was then told that the seat of government in the city was taken over by some gun men who made it very difficult for cars to travel. As a result, we're all locked up this morning until the situation is brought under control. I've therefore used the opportunity to let you know about the uncertainties and risks we face here...
Despite all these however, I'm confident that the Lord works out all things for the good of them who love Him and are called to His purpose. Let's continue to pray that the Lord will complete that which he has already started doing about the furtherance of my schooling in the United States. He's undoubtedly the Alpha and Omega; the author and finisher of our faith. I know that though the road is rough and the journey tough, I shall overcome through your various prayers and support...

Shadrach

In the same group of letters I also received the following communication from Shadrach now in the Ivory Coast.

Danane', Ivory Coast

September 30, 1994

...Because of the unpromising security situation in all of Liberia, including Monrovia, I've been advised by Mrs. Zigbou to return to neighboring Ivory Coast and await the completion of my application procedure. No one is really certain about what will happen in the next few moments, days or weeks as the military and political situation deteriorates daily. This level of uncertainty was even enhanced by the abortive coup of September 15 of which I spoke of in my more recent letter to you...

Shadrach

After these two letters, I knew that I had no concept whatsoever of the difficulties of living in a country as unstable as Liberia. Shadrach and I had by now corresponded enough that I had begun to feel a deep concern for his safety and wellbeing. I felt like I had an adopted son who was trapped in a dangerous situation that I had no control over or ability to change. I expressed my frustration to my pastor one day. "I'm not trying to save the world, David. I only want to save one person and I can't seem to accomplish anything to help." He gently reassured me to be patient that all would work out. All I could do at that point was to push onward more diligently to follow up on the applications Shadrach had sent to US universities. We soon had the choice narrowed down to two, Methodist University in Fayetteville, NC which was close to Mary Zigbou's American relatives and the University of Indianapolis here in Indiana. The University of Indianapolis offered Shadrach a scholarship of 50% tuition but the total tuition/room and board was $16,000 without accounting for the cost of books and other supplies. I didn't have the kind of money needed to pay the balance myself so with the help of my minister, we made a plea to the area Methodist churches for help. The response was overwhelming. We received contributions from Westfield, Danville, Plainfield, Crawfordsville, and Bridgeport United Methodist of Indianapolis. With an additional $2000 grant from the University of Indianapolis we were able to pledge Shadrach's first year of college expenses. This looks easier in retrospect than it was. In reality, we were scrambling to get enough together to convince the US Embassy to give Shadrach a visa so he could start classes the summer session of school 1995. It was hard to believe but nearly two years had passed since my first conversation with Carolyn Wagner. The war in Liberia made communication painfully slow. Every letter took at least a month in transit and phone service was extremely unreliable. With all this working against us though we were now very close to accomplishing the first great hurdle to get Shadrach in college at last.

Chapter 6

Literally a ream of documentation is needed to acquire a student visa from the US Embassy in Monrovia but the document of utmost importance is the I-20. This is the confirmation from the University that all expenses for the first year are committed. Without this it is useless to even attempt to get a visa. During the period that we were trying to get all the financial support lined up so that the University of Indianapolis could send the I-20, Shadrach was waiting in Danane', avoiding the resurgence of fighting in Liberia. On a spring day in the Ivory Coast, a special gift arrived in the mail.

Danane', Ivory Coast

March 19, 1995

Glory to God and may His supreme name be forever praised... Amen! Truly God is good to all His handiwork and His loving kindness is everlasting. He deserves praises more than I've words to offer, and this is because He has heard my prayers, your prayers, my family's prayers, the Church's prayers and all other prayers on my behalf.
This is to inform you that I've received that important I-20 form at last from the University of Indianapolis. It all happened like this: two days ago I received a letter from the continental express agency here in Abidjan asking me to contact them as soon as possible for a parcel they've just received for me. I hurried down that same day from Danane' and after spending roughly a day on the bus arrived in Abidjan the next morning. I then went over to the office of this agency using the address they've given me and there was the I-20 and other important documents.
Meanwhile, be informed that I'll be traveling to Monrovia in less than a week's time (probably at the time you receive this letter) to pursue the visa. After this process we'll get in touch with you from that end to arrange the traveling plan. According to the I-20, I've to arrive on campus no later than May 9, 1995.
Until then, may the Lord richly bless you all and may he make my

stay over in the US a blessed one to the church, to you, the school, my family, all others and me.

Shadrach

By the time I did receive this letter of joy, Shadrach had traveled back to the dangers of Monrovia to the US Embassy there. It would have been safer to go to the embassy in the Ivory Coast but this was not an option since Shadrach was a Liberian citizen and had to apply for his visa in his country of origin. He would later recount his harrowing day at the embassy.

He arrived early in the morning with all the needed documentation that included the I-20, letters of recommendation from his sponsors, and proof of financial support. He waited through the day watching as all the people ahead of him applying for visas left discouraged as they were turned down by the official at the embassy. Finally he was called into the official's office. He silently poured over Shadrach's papers. Satisfied that he had looked over everything, he asked one question. "You were recommended by Methodist missionaries?" Shadrach responded that he was. Without any other comment the embassy official retorted, "Alright, come back tomorrow to pick up your visa." Shadrach was at first speechless but was able to gather himself to thank the man and hurriedly leave the embassy praying that he would not change his mind. He didn't however, for Shadrach was able to pick up his visa the next day, praising God. No one else that day had received a visa but him. Was this official somehow touched by a Methodist missionary in the past so that his heart was softened to Shadrach's case? We may never know. But now the way was finally cleared for Shadrach to make the long journey to the United States.

Chapter 7

The day was finally here. Shadrach was arriving today at Indianapolis International Airport from Liberia after a grueling 17 hr. flight with two plane changes enroute. Needless to say, I was a bit nervous. We had sent numerous letters back and forth from Africa and the United States but we had never actually met. I had so many unanswerable questions. We had developed a strong bond by letters but would it be the same in person? How would Shadrach acclimate to such a different culture than he was used to? Would he actually be able to compete in the US university system? How would my family feel about him once they met him? I'm sure he had all these same questions and more. All I knew was that we would answer them together with God's help. When Shadrach walked off the plane into the airport, Joe and Carolyn Wagner, David and June Owen and my husband and I were waiting. He looked so tired and much too thin but had a great big smile and hugs for all of us. All the usual greetings and questions about his trip passed between us. It was obvious all he really needed right now was a shower and a good night's rest. We headed home to our house outside of Zionsville where my three children anxiously awaited the arrival of our guest from Africa. As we walked into the house, my youngest child Garrett, who was seven years old at the time, rushed down from upstairs calling, "Is Shadrach here, is Shadrach here?" I think he was the one who gave Shadrach the most enthusiastic greeting of all. They were best buddies immediately. Garrett enlisted Shadrach right then and there as an adopted older brother. Whenever he was around our house Garrett was his little shadow. Shadrach never seemed to mind though. I think it helped having Garrett and my two girls, Anna and Rozie around for him not miss his own younger siblings at home quite as much. I really could not imagine being so far away from home like this with strangers. The farthest I had ever stayed for any length of time away from my family was in college at Purdue University. This was no more than an hour from my parents' home. It took a tremendous amount of courage, trust in God and sheer will to achieve the impossible that enabled Shadrach to step out of his own comfort zone to come to the United States. It was also quite a leap of faith for Shadrach's parents to trust total strangers to care for their son. It was in the first year after Shadrach's arrival that I received a letter from his father expressing his feelings.

Liberia, W. Africa

March 18, 1996

Dear Dr. Suzanne Montgomery,

In the name of our Lord Jesus Christ, I take this time to extend my sincere greeting to you which I hope it will meet you in good condition as well as I am asking God to be. I received a fruitful information from my son Shadrach Gonqueh that you are there helping him in everything. Therefore, I extend you my thanks and appreciation for your goodness toward my son Shadrach. I pray to almighty God to continue blessing you for your good work. I do not have anything to give you but the Lord God will pay you for all you are doing for my son. I ask that you may join us in prayer so that God Himself may finish the crisis in our home Liberia so we can get better communication between us. May God richly bless you.

Yours in Christ, Mr. Gonqueh

This letter brought tears to my eyes. How would I feel to send my own children off to places unknown? Would my faith be strong enough to bear the grief of separation even if it was the best thing for my child? Shadrach's father, Johnstone, had to bear the heavy responsibility of keeping his family safe and secure during a violent civil war. People who had once been neighbors or co-worker were now enemies. I know from what Shadrach told me that his parents wanted to stay neutral in the conflict. They often helped people on both sides, a fact that angered many but blessed many others. They had to put their full trust in God for all their needs. Even now Shadrach's father was trusting God that his son would be safe in my hands. It was my responsibility to live up to that trust and try to help Shadrach adjust to his new surroundings as best he could.

Chapter 8

Shadrach was to start summer school at the University of Indianapolis in one week after his arrival. We had much to do to get him ready. We shopped for the usual school supplies recommended by the university plus some new clothes. Shadrach brought very little with him-just a couple pairs of dark pants and long sleeved white shirts. This was an adventure in itself to take him to a place like Wal-Mart. He had never seen so much in one store. It was overwhelming. We did fairly well locating the needed items except in the hair department. He came to me not long after he arrived saying that he needed some things for his hair and skin. His skin was ashy and the shampoo in the bathroom was drying out his hair. I had nothing in the house to help him since I was not accustomed to the different hair and skin needs between Blacks and Caucasians. On a trip back to Wal-Mart, he educated me on what products were useful. We were both in a learning process.

Before Shadrach arrived, I had purchased a large down jacket for him for the coming winter. He started wearing it in September. When I informed him that September in Indiana was not cold compared to the rest of winter, he was aghast. I don't think he thought he would make it through the first winter on campus. Walking out in the weather to classes can be a challenge even for hardy northerners no less someone from near the equator. He told me later that the old people in Liberia would not survive our winters. I'm sure our old people would also have trouble surviving the heat in Liberia. It is so much harder to adjust to new circumstances the older we get. I guess all of us can get set in our ways. I hope I can take this as a life lesson as I age to try my best in the future to be open to change.

Later that first winter over Christmas break, we took a trip with our church up to Pokagon State Park in Angola Indiana. They have a beautiful, Swiss style lodge there and a quarter mile toboggan run. My kids absolutely loved this place. We bundled up to brave the weather for some tobogganing and took Shadrach along. He had already experienced his first snow and had been so excited. Now we all went ice skating on the frozen lake in front of the inn. At first he was a little reluctant but when he saw that it was safe, he joined in. What fun to see him sliding on the ice for the first time. We all died laughing when he exclaimed, "I'm walking on water!" He later became quite concerned about the trees without their leaves. I'm sure that he had learned about deciduous trees losing their leaves in biology class but to see them do this was a whole different thing. "The trees look like they're all dead," he said to me one day. "Believe me. They're not." I assured him. "It's like the resurrection. They will all come back to life in the spring. Just wait." What a beautiful thing to experience spring with Shadrach for the first time. It's really a confirmation of God's promises as each season passes to the next. We so often take it for granted that every year we can trust Him to come through again with a glorious rebirth.

By the time spring came around and school was coming to a close in early May, Shadrach had been with us a year. He was very much a changed person. He had acclimated to American culture with grace. He was as Jesus said, "wise as a serpent and innocent as a dove."[3] He observed all that came to him then decided what to assimilate and what to discard. There is much in American society today to tempt us. We would all be wise to guard our hearts against that which would lead us away from God. Shadrach was able to do this. He could live on campus, interact with the students but still keep his integrity and high moral standard. Because of this the students and faculty loved him. He befriended the president of the university and by the end of his first year he had convinced him to offer his sister, Mary a full scholarship to pursue a nursing degree. He found a sponsor family at the University Heights Methodist Church that adjoins the campus of University of Indianapolis. Soon Mary was on her way from Liberia to join her younger brother in America, pursuing an education her parents could only imagine in a fairy tale. The dream was all coming true for the two that not long ago had fled their country to be refugees in a foreign place.

[3]Matthew 10:16, "The New Oxford Annotated Bible", NRSV 1994

Chapter 9

As the first year came to a close in May 1996, all of my initial questions and fears had been answered. My relationship with Shadrach had only grown deeper since he had arrived. I had become the surrogate American mother while he was away from his own mother, Ruth in Liberia. My children were his American brother and sisters. He even started calling my parents, Grandma and Grandpa. More than a few eyes would turn when he called them this out in public. They didn't care. In their eyes, he was a grandson just like their other two grandsons, Garrett and my nephew, Nick. So my fears that he would not bond with my family were unfounded.
I also was greatly relieved that he was more than capable of competing in an American university. He had all A's except one B in chemistry after his freshman year at University of Indianapolis. That one B really bothered him. He asked me more than once if I thought he should take the class over so he could get an A. "Heavens, no." I said. "One B is more than fine for your first year here. You should be really proud of yourself." We all were extremely proud of his accomplishments.
During this time we still had to worry however, about financing school for the next year. Shadrach did not have a full scholarship so we needed the commitment of the churches to continue to be able to finish his education. He often would speak during Sunday services at these churches to garner support. The first time I ever went with him to one of these speaking engagements was when he spoke at Sheridan First United Methodist in Sheridan Indiana which is very close to our home. He spent Saturday night with us with the plan that the two of us would go to Sheridan the next morning. Shadrach would often study late into the night which he did that night. In the morning I had a hard time getting him awake to go to church. He was on a college student's clock-stay up half the night and sleep in the next morning. This time however, he could not sleep in. As I drove him to the church I couldn't help but think, "How on earth is he going to wake up enough to make a good impression on these people?" Again my question was unfounded. When we arrived at the church and Shadrach went up to the pulpit to speak, it was like a light turned on in him. As he told his story, the audience was riveted on every word. He painted a vivid picture of what life was like in Liberia during the war and how God had protected and directed him to where he was today. He thanked all the people there

for their generosity. He told them that he was blessed to be a blessing. Wow! How did this sleepy young man just captivate the whole audience including me? I've listened to Shadrach speak numerous times since then and I never cease to be amazed. God has given him a wonderful gift to be able to get up in front of groups of people with confidence in himself and the One who created him and speak the truth in a way that motivates people to higher things. I thought then that this ability would either serve him well when he returned to Liberia someday or it could get him in big trouble. Speaking the truth doesn't make a lot of friends in a corrupt political system. He would have to wait to return until the country was much safer than it was at that moment.

Chapter 10

As the next three years passed while Shadrach continued his undergraduate education at the University of Indianapolis, we had the joy of spending many week-ends and family vacations with him. On one such occasion we had traveled to one of our favorite places, Lake Lure in the mountains of North Carolina. Shadrach, the kids and I were wading in a clear, cool mountain stream that emptied into the lake. All of a sudden, we saw a large black snake about 2 feet long near the edge of the stream. Shadrach went after it in attack mode, ready to end the snake's life. "No, no! Don't kill it!" I exclaimed. "It's not a poisonous snake. It's useful for eating the rodents in the area." He backed away from the snake and it slithered away. "Snakes can be very dangerous in my country," he said, and proceeded to tell us a tale involving an encounter with a very large snake when Shadrach was a young boy. At that time in Shadrach's life, his family lived on the Firestone Rubber Plantation. They had a garden they tended to supplement their diet. On this particular day, they were weeding the rice patch. They had machetes to cut down the large overgrowth that was encroaching the garden. Out of the corner of his eye, Shadrach spied a huge snake, a boa constrictor. This very snake had been terrorizing the village by killing small animals. The villagers were worried that it might make one of the little children its next prey. Shadrach sprinted toward the snake as it tried to escape. When he reached the snake he swiftly brought his machete down just behind the snake's head. His machete bounced off the snake's hide barely leaving a mark. The snake now angry, turned and lunged toward Shadrach. He was fast enough to evade the snake's attempts while continuing to slash at the snake. Shadrach's family was screaming for him to run away but he kept on hitting the snake with his machete. He was now injuring the snake and it tried to get away from him. He pursued it until it was dead. Shadrach's father was very upset with him for risking his life but also very thankful that the feared snake was dead. The whole village was ecstatic. Shadrach was the hero of the day as the great snake killer. He told us that this snake was so large that everyone in the village was given a portion of it to eat. At the end of this story, we were all astounded. "Now, how old were you when you killed the snake?" I asked. "Oh, around 12 years old," he said. All I could think of at that moment was that I wasn't sure I ever wanted to go to Liberia if they had snakes that big but if I ever did, I would want to be there with Shadrach, the courageous snake killer.

Chapter 11

Although during our time with Shadrach we were invited numerous times to partake of Liberian food, we were never served snake. I was thankful. Snake was not an item normally on their table but I came to learn that out of need a Liberian never wasted anything. Shadrach was no exception. He was always open to try anything that was set before him and finish it. Everything that is, except jello. I think it was the texture that he couldn't palate. That I could understand. The first time he ever saw pizza he had a very odd look on his face. "What is that?" he asked cautiously with a tone indicating that he wasn't sure about eating whatever it was. "Its pizza," I quipped. "It's the staple of the college student's diet. This you're going to have to get used to."

He did come to like pizza and adjusted to the American diet quite quickly. However, I knew he greatly missed the traditional food from home. When he asked to cook a Liberian meal for us I helped him find the ingredients. A typical meal would have rice and a soup with vegetables and usually chicken. The soup would often be made with palm butter derived from the palm nuts. The first time I witnessed Shadrach adding palm butter to make soup, I was concerned. It reminded me of the lard that my grandmother used to make pie crust years ago when I was a child. I couldn't help but gently say, "This palm butter probably kept you alive in Liberia. However, if you continue to cook with it here along with an already high fat American diet, you're surely going to hurt your heart." I never saw him personally cooking with palm butter again but I'm sure we ate many dishes made with it at Liberian gatherings.

At one such gathering I failed to remember another important bit of information. Liberians like their food hot. They use extremely hot peppers to achieve this. At this particular meal, I unfortunately ingested a habanero pepper hidden in a dish that resembled jambalaya. That was a mistake! The burning began in my mouth then traveled to my esophagus and stomach. Nothing could quench it. I tried water then bread then rice and back to water yet the fire was still blazing. From that time on, I always ask before I eat, "Any hot peppers in this one?"

One especially memorable Liberian meal was held in the home of Dr. David Van Reken, an Indianapolis pediatrician who had served in Liberia as a missionary. He was the sponsor for Shadrach's best friend David Yleah who was also in the United States to study. We and several other Liberian's in the area were invited to feast on Liberian food prepared by Mrs. Van Reken and visit with David who was then in Indianapolis. After the wonderful meal was finished, many gathered out on the screened in porch to talk. I went out too with the intention that I would listen and learn more about Liberia. Unfortunately the conversation quickly turned to politics and it became immediately apparent that there were radically differing opinions in the room. Voices became loud and I began to be afraid the neighbors would soon complain about the uproar. Shadrach however did not raise his voice but talked in an even manner. It wasn't long before he looked over at me and said, "We need to leave now." I fully agreed and ushered my family out to the car quickly. When we were well away, I asked, "What was that all about?" Shadrach explained that the guests were from several different groups in Liberia, some that don't get along well even outside of Liberia. It was obvious that emotions ran deep and hatred was still very fresh. Surely, Dr. Van Renken having spent some time in Liberia would have known that he was inviting people who were enemies back in their homeland. Perhaps he thought that breaking bread together would somehow break down some of the longstanding animosity between these people. That night however, forgiveness and reconciliation were not to happen. We could only hope and pray that with time the anger and hatred would subside so that Shadrach could return someday to a safe, peaceful Liberia.

Chapter 12

It was always a joy to visit with Shadrach's friend David Yleah as we had at the Van Reken's the evening of our Liberian feast. When David was in Indianapolis he would often come up with Shadrach to our home. I knew that David had also lived a hard life in Liberia but no one would ever know it by his demeanor. He radiated the love of Christ in his gentle, kind manner and always had a smile on his face. He was often so quiet that I didn't realize his competitive nature until I played Scrabble with him and Shadrach. I was used to a friendly, relaxed game of Scrabble like I played with my grandmother. The type of game played by this Liberian duo was intense. There were rules that I wasn't aware of and Scrabble words I didn't know existed. I played one game with them and decided I was out of my league. I really don't remember who won most of those hard fought games but I do think they were fairly evenly matched. I could see why they were such good friends. Their personalities complemented each other well. Shadrach was as bold as David was gentle. However they both challenged each other in friendly competitiveness to better themselves.

Both of the young men wanted to be doctors. David had been admitted to a university on Lookout Mountain in Chattanooga, Tennessee. We stopped to visit him another time when Shadrach was vacationing with us in the Smokey Mountains. On the day we arrived, students and parents were there for the new school year's orientation. David had already moved in and was settled. We met him at the Student Union which was extremely crowded with all the newcomers. We decided to have lunch with David there but he needed to return to his dorm room to get something before we could eat. The plan was that we would get a table for all of us in the dining room and wait for his return. As soon as David left, we realized that we had lost track of Garrett in the crowd. He was only 8 years old and was easily hidden in the mass of people milling around. All of us including Shadrach spread out to find him but to no avail. We were ready to contact the campus security when David returned with Garrett in tow. None of us had seen him leave with David. Probably only thirty minutes had passed but it seemed like hours since Garrett had been missing. David and Garrett couldn't understand why we were so upset. Thank goodness Garrett was safely with David! My heart could stop racing now.

I could understand then how Mary and Joseph must have felt when they lost track of Jesus when they were leaving Jerusalem after Passover. The Bible tells us that he was separated from them for three days! They must have been frantic. However when they found him he was calmly studying with the rabbi's in the temple. Their worry was for naught. He was safe in His Father's house. Had I only known that Garrett was with David I would have had no need for worry. But mothers will be mothers throughout the ages and across cultures. We will always worry about our children until they are safely in our arms.

Chapter 13

In Liberia most people walk or use a public bus for transportation. It is unusual to see someone driving a car outside Monrovia. In fact Shadrach said that when Mary Zigbou drove a car in Liberia people stopped and stared. To see a woman driving was unheard of. So it was not surprising that Shadrach didn't know how to drive. In fact, he really had little experience with anything mechanical. At our home, he enjoyed learning how to drive the John Deere to mow the lawn when he was over in the summer. But soon he started asking about learning how to drive a car. We agreed that it would help tremendously if Shadrach could drive up to our home instead of us arranging to transport him back and forth. One of our church members, Mike McDonald who worked in downtown Indianapolis had been picking Shadrach up from school for visits on Friday evening. We would then return him to the university on Sunday evening. This was about a fifty mile round trip each time. In addition, Shadrach had more and more instances when he needed transportation off campus. So it made a lot of sense for him to have his own car. We found out that Mary's sponsors had an old car that they volunteered to give Shadrach. With this information, we decided to enroll him in a local driver training school to get him started. The car would be a gift but it also needed some work before it would be drivable. We traveled down to Mary's sponsors' home to check it out and bring it back to our house for further repairs. It was old and grey but sturdy and solid. It would be perfect for a new driver. It would protect him if he happened to have an accident and no one would care if it acquired a few scratches and dents. We immediately christened it "The Shad-mobile." The name stayed with the old, grey car until it finally gave up and was taken to the auto graveyard. During its time it served Shadrach well.

The first time Shadrach drove it on his own was the same day he received his driver's license. He and his sister, Mary decided they would go to Good Will to shop. They entered onto 465 which is the bypass that circles Indianapolis. Now Shadrach knew the way back and forth from our house but going to Good Will was another thing altogether. He forgot which exit he needed to take so he and Mary circled around the city totally lost. He called me from a gas station for help. After a long conversation, with Mary crying in the background, I had Shadrach headed back home. They were worn out and almost out of gas. The trip to Good Will would wait for another day. I bought Shadrach a detailed map of Indianapolis that day. I gave it to him the next time I saw him and recommended strongly that he keep it in the car at all times.

We all are in need of maps now and again to lead us in the right direction. Without them we would be continually wandering around in circles like Shadrach and Mary that day. Isn't it the same with the Bible? Most of us forget that it is the ultimate map to keep us going in the right direction. During the war in Liberia many books were destroyed including bibles. We had a collection through Operation Classroom to send bibles to Liberia before I knew anything about Shadrach. He received one of those bibles from Indiana with an inscription and picture inside from the donor. Wouldn't you know Shadrach met the woman who sent him his bible at a church where he was speaking? He recognized her from her picture. What an amazing God "coincidence"!

Chapter 14

Shadrach continued to study diligently at the university and his grades reflected his hard work. By the end of his junior year, he was readying himself for medical school. He sat for the MCAT (the Medical College Admission Test) and sent out applications to medical schools including Indiana University Medical School here in Indianapolis. He wasn't overly happy with his MCAT scores but his GPA from the University of Indianapolis was excellent so our hopes were high. The next step was the interview process. He was asked to interview at Indiana University (IU) which was quite encouraging. After his interview began the long waiting process to hear whether he was granted a spot in next year's class.

Time for graduation was approaching and still no word from IU yet. Shadrach's mother, Ruth was able to obtain a visa to come for the graduation. Her arrival began a joyous celebration. An auntie from Liberia who was in Indianapolis also came for the ceremony. Both of the ladies came in colorful traditional Liberian dress. After all the long speeches were done and the diplomas were dispensed, we gathered outside the gym. Shadrach's mother began to sing and dance with sheer joy. After all the trials and literally fighting for her family to survive, she had witnessed her first child graduating from college. This was a day like no other. She sang praises to God giving Him thanks for all that He had done and would do in the future. Rock solid faith is born out of fire and Ruth's faith was an example of this. Shadrach and Mary longed to hold on to their mother but soon the time on her visa had run out and she had to return to Liberia. There were tearful good-byes all around as she departed on her long journey back home.

As summer wore on, Shadrach's anxiety increased more and more. Unfortunately, I knew that a last minute admission was unlikely. It was difficult to stay positive and not be discouraged. Finally Shadrach did hear something from IU but it was not an offer of admission as a first year medical student. He and half a dozen other students were asked to participate in preparatory studies for IU Medical School. The program was called a Masters in Medical Science. The students were promised admission to the medical school either after the first or second year of study if they did well. Shadrach jumped at the chance thinking that this was surely his ticket in to med school. During the next two years he studied along with the medical students taking many of the same classes. This included human anatomy where he was able to dissect a human cadaver. His stories from this class brought back many old memories of constantly smelling like formaldehyde. Shadrach thoroughly enjoyed his studies and I was encouraged that soon he would be joining the other medical students.

However, this was not to be. After the first and then the second year of the masters program, none of the students who participated gained admission to the IU Medical School. Shadrach was devastated. Why would they promise admission if they never intended to grant it? He went to the admissions office asking what more he could do. At that point he was told that because he was an international student he had to obtain a permanent resident visa to be admitted. He had always had a student visa and was never told prior to this that changing his visa was necessary. He vigorously set forth to apply for his permanent resident visa. He sent all the necessary documentation to the INS (Immigration and Naturalization Service) and waited for their response. Months went by with no answer. Shadrach would call intermittently and was told that it was being processed. I called one of our US Senators for assistance but received no response. The final blow came on September 11, 2001. With the destruction of the Twin Towers in New York City by terrorist, we knew it would be nearly impossible to obtain the needed visa.

During this time of waiting, I had advised Shadrach to acquire a job in health care to stay in touch with the medical field. He did some training at Wishard Hospital on the IU Medical Center campus to be an endoscopy tech. He then worked there with the IU gastroenterologist and then later at St. Francis Hospital on the south side of Indianapolis. He continued diligently to obtain the permanent resident visa but to no avail.

Why would God open so many doors for Shadrach to let them all slam shut now? What was the point? I couldn't understand this at all. Hadn't he gone through enough already and wasn't his dream to help his people a valid one? Shadrach was discouraged but I was mad. Mad at the system that shut him out and mad at God. Even yet, I prayed and prayed but no answer to Shadrach's dilemma came forth. In my heart however, I kept hearing "Trust Me." Even though nothing made sense, I chose to trust that God was equipping Shadrach for something important. Maybe it just wasn't time yet to reveal it.

Chapter 15

By the summer of 2003 we had virtually given up on Shadrach ever entering medical school. He had applied to numerous schools but was turned down always for the same reason-he had no permanent resident visa. Immigration had tightened down so much after 9/11 that Shadrach was given no hope of obtaining this type of visa anytime in the near future. It was then that his attention was suddenly turned in a completely different direction. Shadrach had come to visit one week-end as he often did, but this time he had something serious to discuss with me. He hadn't given me any idea what this was but I could tell it was important. He started out by saying, "I hope you're not going to think I'm crazy but I've had a very troubling dream I need to talk to you about." He then proceeded to tell me his unusual dream.

"I was back in Liberia and a large group of people were all lined up waiting to see me. I asked them what they needed and they each in turn replied that they were there for various dental problems. I told them that I couldn't help them because I wasn't a dentist but they would not leave. At that moment, my father came up beside me holding a large document. He told me that I was a dentist and he held out the document that was a diploma from dental school with my name on it. I told him that this could not be. I wanted to be a medical doctor not a dentist. But he insisted that it was true. I somehow was a dentist. I then started to treat all the people who had been waiting and I miraculously knew how to help them." When Shadrach finished I was silent for a few moments. I could tell the dream had confused and grieved him. It had not been long since he had heard from Liberia that his father had suddenly taken ill and died. I knew he was still not healed from this. After this silence he added, "My father seemed so proud of me in the dream." Then he asked, "Do you think this dream means anything?"

I would say that in most instances, dreams are simply a fantasy world of our own mind. But I also believe that certain dreams have deeper meaning. Shadrach knew that I had had a few dreams in the past of this sort. From my experience, the person dreaming knew intuitively that this type of dream was more than fantasy. I had felt before like Joseph with his coat of many colors who knew without a doubt that his dreams were messages from God.

"Did you sense that this dream was different from your other dreams?" I asked.

"Definitely."

"You know that I believe that some dreams are actually messages from God. Do you feel that God is perhaps trying to redirect you with this dream?" Shadrach paused deep in thought. "Yes, I think He could be. You know that my friend, Dave Judy who is a dentist has often spoken to me about considering dentistry. I was so focused on pursuing medical school that I didn't even consider it."

"Well, I'm sure that dentists are needed just as much in Liberia as medical doctors. Are they not?"

"Oh yes, certainly. One of my sisters suffered terribly with an infected tooth for months before she could find a dentist to treat her. A dentist would be very busy in Liberia."

"Are you going to look into the possibility of dental school?"

"Do you think I should?"

"Shadrach, I believe if this is the direction God wants you to go, He will make it abundantly clear. I would go for it if you think it is the right thing and see what happens."

Soon after our conversation, Shadrach made a trip to the IU dental school office of admissions to ask questions. The most important question was whether they required a permanent resident visa as had all the medical schools. To his relief they did not. A student visa was acceptable. They seemed openly receptive of international students in contrast and encouraged him to send them his transcripts. To be considered he also would need to sit for the dental admissions test. They gave him information about how to sign up for this before he left.

Shadrach was ecstatic. This was so different than what he had experienced with the medical schools. Whereas he had been treated as if he wasn't good enough before, now he felt welcomed. In short order, he was able to take his admission test and did quite well. He went through the interview process and soon received his letter of admission to IU dental school for the fall of 2004. Doors that had been closed were now open wide. What had seemed hopeless was now becoming a reality. The circumstances were not as he had originally imagined but nevertheless, Shadrach was going to be a doctor!

Chapter 16

It wasn't long after Shadrach was admitted to the IU Dental School that we began to realize financing his studies was going to be much more difficult than it was for his undergraduate degree. For one thing, dental school was much more expensive than the University of Indianapolis. Tuition and books would run around $25,000 to $30,000 per year. Then there were living expenses. Shadrach was still working at St. Francis Hospital but once school started the curriculum would be too intense for him to even work part-time. Unlike the University of Indianapolis there were no scholarships available that we could find. Luckily Shadrach did qualify for guaranteed student loans. These would act as a safety net if we couldn't generate enough money from the local churches that had helped Shadrach before. Two churches came forward that contributed substantially during this time. They were St. Luke's United Methodist and Zionsville United Methodist. Both of these churches are located on the north side of Indianapolis, have large congregations and have strong commitments to missions. They stood faithfully beside Shadrach throughout his four years in dental school. God chose to put two people in particular in our path that would become good friends and mentors for Shadrach. Kay and Gary Walla are members of St. Luke's and greatly encouraged their church to support Shadrach. We first met them on a mission trip to San Antonio Texas in the late 90's. Again we worked with them on a medical mission to Haiti in 2000. The Walla's, my mother and Shadrach ran the make shift pharmacy there while I saw patients with the other doctors and nurse practitioners in our group. This trip was quite an awakening for Shadrach. He hadn't thought that any people were in as much need as the Liberians. But by the end of our mission, he felt that the Haitians were in even a more desperate situation. He was thankful that we were able to go there to help the little bit that we did. During this experience he developed a strong relationship with the Walla's that continued after our return. Their assistance was indispensible as Shadrach readied himself for dental school.

Over the years he spent in the United States, Shadrach made numerous friendships but the one that would become his most significant relationship happened again through letters out of Africa. The year prior to his admission to dental school he began corresponding with a young Liberian woman who was a friend of his family. Her name was Ruby. She lived in

Monrovia and from what Shadrach told me I knew that she enjoyed swimming at the beach, she loved dogs and helped to care for some of the many orphans from the war. They had written back and forth for some time so I was not surprised when he told me that he wanted to return to Liberia over Christmas to visit her. He had made other trips back home since he came to the US but it wasn't often due the great expense of travel to Africa and the length of time it took to get to Liberia. He had enough vacation time to stay for almost 3 weeks. He told me that he wanted to determine if Ruby was the one he would want to marry. He went with the expectation that if all went well he would ask her hand in marriage before he returned to the US. He was only there a short time when I received an urgent email from him. The internet was much more available in Monrovia now so Shadrach was able to find a computer to send this message. He asked me what I thought if he were to get married while he was in Liberia. Apparently his family and Ruby's family had planned a wedding for him and Ruby. They just failed to tell him that before he arrived. Everything was ready. All he needed was a ring for Ruby.

I knew that Shadrach cared very much for Ruby but I also could tell he felt a little pressured. Arranged marriages are a common occurrence in most of the world but in the US this is rarely done anymore. My first inclination was to tell him that he should just get engaged as he had planned and give the relationship some time before the wedding. However, it was clear that this was not the desire of their families. The best advice I could give him was to pray and then follow his heart. His marriage would succeed if God was placed in the center of it.

Shadrach and Ruby were married just after the new year on January 4th, 2004. She was unable to obtain a visa so did not join him in the US for nearly 6 months. When she arrived she enrolled in nursing school at the University of Indianapolis. Both she and Shadrach started school the fall of 2004. On Valentine's Day 2006, their first child, Abigail was born and two years later their son Nathan decided to arrive the morning of his father's graduation from dental school. As Shadrach was receiving his diploma, Ruby was in the hospital recovering from delivering their child. The Walla's, my parents and I were present for the graduation ceremony. There had been many roadblocks along the way that had discouraged Shadrach from his goal but one thing was apparent throughout all the years. God's hand was working always in and through the many people who helped Shadrach along the way. God knew the path He had for Shadrach but it was God's timing as to when and how this path would be revealed. As it says in the book of Jeremiah, "For surely I know the plans I have for you, says the Lord, plans for your welfare and not for harm, to give you a future with hope. Then when you call upon me and come and pray to me, I will hear you. When you search for me, you will find me; if you seek me with all your heart. I will let you find me, says the Lord, and I will restore your fortunes and gather you from all the nations and all the places where I have driven you, says the Lord, and I will bring you back to the place from which I sent you into exile."[4] As a refugee, Shadrach came to the United States. He was an exile from his own country. Surely God has plans to complete the work that He has started in Shadrach and return him home to Liberia with hope in his heart for the renewal of his people. Shadrach's graduation was only the beginning of the next chapter in the unfolding of God's grace in his life. I am so thankful that God chose to invite me to be a part of His plan. What if I had said no to His prompting those many years ago when Carolyn Wagner came to speak at my church? I feel sure that God would have found another way to carry out His plan for Shadrach. However, I would have never experienced the richness of the wonderful friendship that God had planned for me. Thank you, God for choosing me to be a part of this story.

[4] Jeremiah 29:11-14, "The Oxford Annotated Bible", 1994.

Epilogue

It is now 2013 and Shadrach is working diligently to repay his student loans so he and his family can return to Liberia. He presently is practicing dentistry in Indianapolis. Ruby is finishing her degree in nursing. Her studies were delayed with the birth of now three children, Abigail, Nathan and Naomi. The political situation in Liberia appears to be more stable. Shadrach tells me that the people are tired of war and are ready for peace. I pray that he is right. Shadrach is in the process of building a house that will also serve as his dental clinic in Liberia in preparation for bringing the family there soon. Ruby took the children to Liberia on more than one occasion to see their grandparents and extended family. I'm sure both grandmothers sang with joy at the sight of these 3 beautiful grandchildren. I commended Ruby on her courage. To take three young children on such a long journey is very brave indeed. The fact that she felt comfortable traveling back to Liberia speaks to the fact that it is safe to be there now.

God's timing is always perfect. He has kept Shadrach here until the situation was right for him to return. Rebuilding efforts are going on in Liberia to help the people recover from the devastating civil war. Shadrach and several of his Liberian friends have started a Christian college in Ganta, Liberia and have graduated 2 classes already. Groups like Hope in the Harvest are teaching Liberians to farm so they can feed their families and sell crops for income. The process of healing is well underway. When Shadrach is ready to start his dental clinic in Liberia, there are many here in the US prepared to help him. The Walla's have a fund started to buy dental equipment for the clinic and my son Garrett is prepared to physically help Shadrach get it to Liberia.

God has set the groundwork. Now the next chapter in Shadrach's story is ready to begin.

Acknowledgement

I wish to thank all those who played key roles in this story for their faithfulness and perseverance: Carolyn and Rev. Joe Wagner, Rev. David VW Owen, Mary and Rev. Herbert Zigbuo, Kay and Gary Walla, Dr. Dave Judy, and Mike McDonald. I am greatly indebted to them for their undying support of Shadrach throughout his journey. Thank you to all the many churches in the Indianapolis area who helped with his financial needs. Last but not least I thank my family for standing by me and loving Shadrach like a brother.

Above all, I want to give credit to God who through His grace chose to introduce Shadrach to me and guided us on an adventure that has yet to be completed. None of this would have happened without You.

Study Questions

1. In the beginning of "Letters Out of Africa," I describe a sense that God wanted me to do more but I didn't know what. Have you ever felt restlessness in your soul like this? If so, what did you do about it?

2. Throughout the book God made Himself known in many different ways. He miraculously protected Shadrach in several dangerous situations. He spoke to me through a deep, inner voice. He directed Shadrach through a dream. What other ways have you experienced God in your own life? How did these experiences make you feel?

3. God often asks us to step out of our comfort zones. Inviting a refugee from Africa into my home was way out of mine. How has God asked you to step out in faith? Were you surprised by what happened when you did?

4. Shadrach's goal was to become a medical doctor but this didn't happen. Have you ever had an instance when you thought you were going in the right direction with your life only to have road blocks at every turn? Did it force you to take another course or did you push on anyway?

5. In the story I became angry with God when circumstances out of our control put Shadrach's career goals on hold. I felt that God had lead Shadrach so far then let him down. Do you think it's ok to be angry with God? How best do you handle these feelings?

6. Shadrach and I came from two very different cultural backgrounds yet our basic values were the same. How do you think that was so? Has this been your experience when your life has intersected with someone of a different culture or race? If not, what were the most difficult obstacles to overcome in your relationship with that person?

Resources

For more information about groups that are helping the Liberian people to recover from the civil war go to:
http://www.hopeintheharvest.org and http://www.operationclassroom.org

About the Author

Suzanne Montgomery is a Family Physician practicing in the Indianapolis area for the last 26 years. She has been involved in mission work locally through free clinics as well as international medical missions in Haiti and Ecuador. She was introduced to Dr. Shadrach Gonqueh through missionaries when he was a refugee of the Liberian civil war studying in an Operation Classroom school in the Ivory Coast. The book "Letters Out of Africa" was conceived from the many letters between Suzanne and Shadrach over a 2 year period as he struggled to stay alive while waiting to travel to the US to become a doctor.

She presently is working as a staff physician for Indiana University Health in Indianapolis. She lives with her husband, 2 cats and a dog in an old farmhouse north of the city surrounded by corn and bean fields. Her 3 grown children and 3 step children all live locally. She has a large vegetable garden at her home and enjoys tending this as well as hiking the many beautiful Indiana State Parks.

She can be contacted at: lettersoutofafrica@yahoo.com or www.lettersoutofafrica.com

Letters Out of Africa

Copyright ©2011 by Suzanne Elaine Montgomery
Book cover design and author photograph by Anna Montgomery.
Landscape photograph by Dan Lutes.
No part of this book may be used or reproduced in any manner whatsoever without permission except in the case of brief quotations embodied in critical articles or reviews.

www.ingramcontent.com/pod-product-compliance
Lightning Source LLC
Chambersburg PA
CBHW061345040426
42444CB00011B/3100